W. S. Merrill

Private receipts, 1878

W. S. Merrill

Private receipts, 1878

ISBN/EAN: 9783742823267

Manufactured in Europe, USA, Canada, Australia, Japa

Cover: Foto ©Gila Hanssen / pixelio.de

Manufactured and distributed by brebook publishing software
(www.brebook.com)

W. S. Merrill

Private receipts, 1878

℞

Aqua Cinnamon
Alcohol
Syrup Simplex
Aqua Purae aa
Tinct Auranti Cort
Tinct Cardamon aa
M

Cerate Acid Carbolici

℞

Acid Carbolic grs v
Cerate Simplex ℥i
M

Suppositories of Acid
℞

Acid Tannic grs XXXvi
Adipis Benzo grs CX
Ol Theabrom grs CCXX
Cera Alb grs XXXV
ft suppos No XII

Cough Mixture

℞

Vini Ipecac ℥i

Tinct Opii Camph ℥ß

Camphorae ʒi

Saccharum

Aqua Purae aa ℥iv

M.

Sig Teaspoonful three ti[mes]
a day.

Cough Mixture D

℞

Syr Scillae mae

Syr Senegae aa ℥i

Vin Antimonii ℥ß

Tinct Opii Camph ʒij

M

Cough Mixture

℞

Morph Sulph grs iij

Potass Iodid ʒi

Vin Antimonii ʒi

Glycerin opt

Syr Tolutani aa ℥ij

M

Sulphur Lactis ʒij
Plumbi Acet ʒi
Glycerinae ℥i
Aqua ℥ij
Aquae Cologne ℥i
M

Hair Wash

℞
Oleum Ricini ℔s ijss
Alcohol O ijss
Pulv Cantharides ℥ss
Ol Bergami ℥ss
Ol Rosae gtts x
M
Macirate 4 days.

Hot Drops
(Tinct Myrrhae et Capsici

℞
Pulv Myrrhae ℥iv
" Capsici ℥ij
Alcohol O iv
M
Mac. dies vii

Mixture for Gonorrhoea
Dr Warren

℞

Copaiva	℥i
Ol Cubebae	℥ij
Tr Opii	ʒi
Mucil Acaciae	℥ij
Spts Aeth Nit	℥ss
Spts Lavand Co	ʒiij
Aqua Camph (℥iv)	℥[illegible]
Saccharum	ʒij
Ol Gaultheriae	gtts x

M ft Mist

Sig: Tablespoonful three or four times a day.

Mixture

℞.

Copaibae	℥i
Pulv Cubebae	℥ij
Ol Menth Pip	gtts xxx

M

Signa. Doze a peice as larg as a nutmeg twice a day.

Hair Dye

No 1.

℞.

Acid Gallici grs XX

Alcohol ℥ij

Aqua ℥vi.

M

No. 2. Dye

℞

Argenti Nitras ʒij

Aqua Dist ℥vi

Aqua Ammon fort qs.

M

Horse Liniment

℞

Oleum Origani

" Olive

Aqua Ammon Fort aa

Alcohol ℥xij

M

Tinct Serpentaria Comp
Dr Bascom

℞
Rad Serpentaria ℥i
Saffron ℥ß
Opium ℥i
Camphor ʒii
Holland Gin Oi
M macerate 14 days

Syr Rhei Comp. Dr Bascom
℞
Rad Rhei contus ℥iv
Golden Seal ℥ß
Capsicum grs XV
Spts Vini Gallice Oii
Mix macerate 2 days then filter
Sig Brandy Tincture
℞
Saccharum lbs ii
Aqua Oiii
Bi-Carb Potass ʒii
heat until disolved then add the Brandy Tinct and 1½ ozs Ess Peppermint.

Tooth Ache Drops

℞
Chloroform
Oil Cloves
Creasote equal parts.

Diarrhae Mist

℞
Tinct Opii
" Capsici
Aether Chloric equal parts
M
Teaspoonful every 4 hours.
then a laxitive. (Dr Crosby Con

Scratch Ointment

℞
White Lead
Adipe aa ℥ i ß
Pulv Alum ℥ ß
Calomel ℈ grs v
25 M

For cementing Iron

Make a paste of Litharg &
Glycerine

711

Lotion for Sore Nipples

℞

Pulv Borax ʒij
Chalk ʒi
Spts of Wine ℥ij
Water ℥iv
M

For Nausea. Depression and craving for drink

℞

Tr Capsici gtts X
Tr Nux Vom gtts X
Acid Nitric dilute gtts XX
Aqua ℥i
M Sig Take as a draught in water 3 or 4 times a day

From the Medical Brief Jan 1875.

For Impotency. to promote erections

℞

Strychnia Sulph grs i
Quinia Sulph ʒß

Lotion for Poison by Ivy

℞

Bromine	gtts x to xx
Glycerine, or Cosmoline	℥ i

M

Apply gently 3 or 4 times a day.
Dr Brown U.S.N. in Druggist Circular
Sept 1878

Mistura Ferri Comp (~~Dr [illegible]~~)

℞

Pulv Myrrhae	
Ferri Sulph aa	ʒ ii
Potass Bi-carb	ʒ i
Ol Mentha Pip	gtts vi
Syrup Simplex	
Aqua Cinnam aa	℥ ii
Aqua	O i

M

Rub the Oil Pip with ½ oz Sugar then with the Myrrh etc then add the Syrup
Dose - Two tablespoonfuls three times a day.

℞
Ol Bitter Almonds
Alcohol
Aqua
M et filter through Magnes

Thompsonian Composition
℞
Pulv Zingiber
" Myrrh
" Capsici
M

Hair Wash to prevent the hair from ;

℞
Ol Ricini
" Bergamot
Pulv Camphor
Alcohol
Aqua Ammon
Tr Cantharides
Aqua Cologne
M

Essences.

		alcohol
Ol Gaultheria	℥ß	Oj
" Rosae	ʒij	"
" Wormwood	℥ß	"
" Carum	ʒij	"
" Limon	℥i	"
" Sassafras	℥ss	"
" Menth Vir	"	"
" " Pip	℥i	"
" Bergamot	"	"
" Cinnamo	℥ß	"
" Anise	"	"

℞	
Bals Copaira	℥ij
Aqua Ammonia	℥ij
Aqua Purae	℥xiv
M	
Shake together Copaira. Ammonia and Aqua ℥iv. then add Aqua	℥x

Mistura Camphora:

℞	
Pulv Camphor	℥ii & grs 8
" Acacia	
" Saccharum aa	℥ß
Aqua Purae	Oj
M	

Liniment Origani

℞

Ol Olivae
Aqua Ammonia
Tinct Opii
Ol Origani. equal parts
M

Cream of Lillies

℞
Potass Carb
Alcohol dil
Ol Bergamot
" Lemon
" Cassia
" Ricini
M

Pil Podophylli
℞
Pil Hydrarg
Ext Podoph
Pul Aloe Soc
M dir in pil No 96

Godfrey's Cordial

℞
Sugarhouse Mollasses
Aqua — aa
Alcohol
Tr Opii
Ol Sassafras
" Juniper
M

℞

Oleum Aurantii	gtts	25
Alcohol	℥ viii	
Magnesia Carb	℥ ii	
Syrup Simp	℥ x	
Sherry Wine	℥ 65	
Ferri Ammo Cit	℥ v - grs	
Ext. Beef (Liebigs)	℥ i ß	

add the oil to the Magnesia. the Alcohol to the wine, and filter the whole slowly through the Magnesia. then add the Syrup.— Solve the Ext of Beef in the wine and syrup. Then dissolve the Iron in hot water. (as little as possible and add that. then add Wine enough to make 5 pts.

Aqua Rosae

℞

Ol Rosae	gtts	vi
Magnes Carb	℥ i	
Aqua	Oj	

M et filtra

Cologne.

℞

Alcohol	O viii
Agua	O i
Ol Rosmary	ʒ ij
" Burgamii	
" Lemon	
" Lavand aa	℥ ss
" Cinnam	
" Caryoph	
" Citronella	
" Cajuput aa	ʒ i
Tinct Musk (opt)	ʒ i
M	

let stand 14 dies et filtra

Dr Little's Ointment

℞

Ung Stramonii	℥ i ss
Zinci Oxid	
Hydrarg Ammon aa	℈ ii
M	

℞
Pulv Camphorae
" Saccharum aa ℥i
" Ipecac
" Glycyrrhizae aa ʒviii
M

Mechanic's Court Plaster

℞
Ichthyocolla (americana) ℥viii
Frozen Glue " i
Tr Benzoin Comp " i
M & strain through cotton or Flannel
Boiling Water O iij

Eye Wash

℞
Zinci Sulph grs xii
Sassafras (med) ℥i
Aqua Rosae ℥vi
M

Dr Reynolds Boston

To produce Sleep.

℞		
Sodii Bromid	℥ i	
Syr Tolu		
Aqua aa	℥ iv	
M		
Tablespoonful at night & repeat until sleep is produced (once in 2 hours) Dr Albert Day		
Condition Powder (for Horses)		
℞		
Antimonii Nig	℥ iv	
Fennigreek	℥ ii	
Potass Nit	℥ iv	
Sulphur	℥ iii	
Sal Epsom	℥ iv	
Liniment for Sprains		
℞		
Ol Origani		
" Cedar		
" Spike		
Aqua Ammon equa parts		
M Rufus Welch		

Silver Plating Fluid

℞ 1 teaspoonful Cream Tartar
½ oz Nit Silver (crystals)
1 " Cyanuret Potassa
8 " Whiting
1 " Fine Salt
M Aqua 1½ pts

Pomade

℞
Ol Ricini
Ol Oliv
Cera alba aa ℥ i
Cetaceum ℥ ss
Tr Cantharides gtts xv
Ol Limonis ℥ i
M

Tooth Powder

℞ Cretae ppt ℥ viii
Pulv Bole Armen ℥ i
Pulv Iris Flor ℥ ij
M
Scent with Wintergreen

Eye Water

℞
Zinci Sulph grs viii
Aqua Dest ℥ ij
Vini Opii ʒ i
M

Bed Bug Poison

℞
Camphor ℥ ij
Ol Terebinth ℥ iv
Hydrarg Cor Chl ʒ i
Alcohol O j
M

Mixture Cod Liver Oil

℞
Ol Morrhuae ℥ xii
Tr Cinchon Comp
Tr Cinnam Comp aa ℥ ij
M

℞

Plumbi Acet
Pulv Opii aa ℈i
Pulv Gallae ʒii
Cerate Simplex ℥i
M

℞

Pulv Gallae ʒi
Plumbi Acet ʒss
Pulv Opii ℈i
Acid Tannic grs x
Adeps ℥ii
M

Wash for Inflamation

℞

Pulv Ammonia Mur ʒi
Alcohol
Acid Acet dilut aa ℥i
Aqua Oj
M

℞

Cetaceum
Ol Oliv a a ℥ vi
Cera Alb ℥ iss
Glycerine
Camphor a a ℥ i
M

Diarrhoe Mixture

℞

Tinct Opii
" Capsici
" Camphor
" Rhei
Spts Menth Pip aa
M
Dose 18 drops every 4 hou

Chloroform Liniment

℞

Tr Sapon Camph ℥
Chloroform ℥ i
Tr Opii ℥ ij
M

℞
Gro Gentian
Quassia
Aurantii Cort aa ℥ss
Anisum
Carum
Soda Bi-carb aa ℥ii
Spirit O i ss
M

Liniment Dr Gross

℞
Chloroform ℥i
Tr. Sapon et Opii aa ℥iij
M

Tr Sapon Camph et Opii

℞
Tr Opii ℥ij
Tr Sapon Camph ℥vi
M

℞

Antimonii Nig
Potass Bi-tart
Pulv Sanguinar
Sulphur Sub a a ℥ i
Potass Nit
Pulv Anise a a ℥ ij
M

Myrrh Mixture (Dr T
℞

Pulv Myrrh ℥ i
Ferri Sulph ℥ ij
Sal Aratus ℥ ß
Ol Cinnam gtts xx
Saccharum Alb ℥ iss
Alcohol ℥ ij
Aqua Pura ℥ xii

Rub the Sugar, Oil Cinna
and Sal aratus with the
then with Aqua ℥ viii.
Rub the Ferri Sulph with
mix the solutions and co
immediately.

Tinct Senna Comp

℞
Senna contused ℥ xiv
Carum ℥ xiv
Cardamon ℥ ss
Raisins deprived of seeds ℥ iv
Alcohol dilut 5 qts
M. macerate 7 days

Unguent Auri Comp (for the Itch)

℞
Potass Carb ℥ ss
Aqua Rosae ℥ i
Hydrarg Sulph Rub ℈ ij
Ol Lavander ℥ i
Sulphur Sub ℥ x
Adeps ℔ i
M

White Gun Powder

℞
Potass Chlorat grs 98
" Prussiate " 36
Sugar " 46
M with care

Colors for Show Bottles.

Green

℞
Cupri Sulph ℔ 1½
Tr Mur Iron ℥ss
Salt ℔s 2½
Aqua 1 gall
M et filter then add Acid Mur

Orange

℞
Potass Bichrom ℥iv
Acid Nitric ℥i
Cochineal ℥i
Alum ℥ss
Acid Sulph ℥i
Aqua 1 gall
M

Tooth Ache Drops

℞
Creasote
Chloroform
Tinct Opii aa ℥i
Tinct Benzoin Comp ℥i
M

Liniment — Dr Snow.

℞
Ol Olive
Ol Terebinth aa ℥ iv
Aqua Ammonia ℥ ij
Tr Sapon Camph ℥ xii
M

Citrate Magnesia
℞
Acid Citric ℥ viii
Aqua O vi
M et Solve

℞
Magnesia Carb ℥ iv
Aqua O ij
M

Mix the two solutions then add Saccharum ℥ viii.
just before corking the bottles add Potass Bicarb ʒ i to each bottle.
Steam the corks so as to have them perfectly tight.

Tinct Gentian Comp.

℞
Rad Gentian No 40. 1 ℔ 2 ℥ Adv
" Aurantii " ℥ix
" Cardamon ℥ 4¼
" Santalum ℥ 2¼
Alcohol dil 2 galls & 20 ℥
Pack in a percolator and
displace 2 galls

Hair Dye

No 1
℞
Acid Gallic ʒß
Alcohol ℥i
Rain Water ℥ij
dissolve the acid in the Alcohol
then add the water

No 2
℞
Argenti Nit ʒi
Aqua Ammonia ʒiij
Acacia Gran ʒß
[illegible]r the silver in the Ammon. do not cork until the
[illegible]re is disolved. Solve the Acacia in ¾ ℥ Rain water
then mix the two solutions

Cough Mixture

℞

Syr Scillae
Syr Senega aa ℥i
Vini Antimonii ʒ ii
Tr Lobelia ʒij
Tr Opii Camph ʒi
M

Andersons Scots Pills

℞

Aloes grs 60
Sapon " 10
Colocynth
Gambogo aa 3grs
Ol Anisi gtts 3
M ft Pill No 24

New England Tooth Ache.

℞

Rad Pyrethrum ʒ viii
Capsicum ʒi
Alchohol Oiv
Chloroform ʒiv
M

℞
Tinct Opii
Tinct Camphorae
Tinct Myrrhae et Capsici
Tinct Rhei
Syr Acacia a a
Tinct Catechu
M
Shake before using. Dose teaspoonful.

Dr White's Dentifrice
℞
Cretae Pup
Pulv Sapo alb
Pulv Camphorae
Ol Gaultheria q s
M Rub through a seive

Bay Rum
℞
Oil Bayberry tree
Jamaica Rum
Alcohol
Aqua
Mix Rum. Alco & water then add Oil et filter

℞

Copaiva	℥i
Sp Nitre	℥ss
Liq Potass	℥ii
Tr Opii	[illegible]
Sy Gaulth	[illegible]
Tr Cubebs	[illegible]
Aq Camph	[illegible]
Mucil Acacia	℥iii

M

2 teaspoonfuls twice a day

Gonor Mixture (June)

℞

Copaiva	℥iii
Fl Ext Cubebs	℥ii
Pulv Aluminis	ʒi
Sacch Alb	ʒii
Mucil Acacia	[illegible]
Aqua	℥ii

M

Teaspoonful 3 or 4 times a day

75¢

A.P.C.

Horse Liniment

1 pt Alcohol
1 oz Ol Origanum
½ " Camphor
½ " Aqua Ammon
½ " Oil Spike
½ " " Cedar
1 ℥ Capsicum.
Levi Johnson's receipt

For Sore teats on Cows
℞
Goulard's Ext	℥ ii
Zinci Sulph	ʒ ii
Adipis	℥ iii

M

Dr White's Dentifrice
℞
Cretae Prep	i-5
Sapo Pulv	i
Pulv Camphor	℥ vi ʒ ss
Ol Gaulther	q.s.

M rub through sieve

Soap Liniment

℞

Soap in shavings	℥ iv Tro
Agua	℥ XIV
Camphor	℥ ii Tr
Ol Rosmar	℥ ß
Alcohol	O i ß

Mix Agua with 8 ℥ Alcohol add the soap and mix with agitation. Solve Camphor and Oil Rosmar in the remainder of Alcohol mix the two solutions and filter.

Elixir Guarana (W.F.S)

℞

Pulv Guarana	℥ iv
Alco dilut q.s.	
make 8 ℥ Tinct. then add	
Agua	℥ ii
Syr Simp	℥ vi
Spts Auranti	℥ ii
" Cinnam	♏ X

M

Elix Pyrophos Ferri (W.F.S)

℞
Ferri Pyrophos — grs 25
Aqua Dist — ℥ i
Simp Elix — ℥ x
M

Bitter Wine of Iron (W.F.S)

℞
Ferri et Quinia Cit — grs 12
Spts Auranti — ℥ ii
Syrup Simp — ℥ i
Sherry Wine — ℥
M

Simple Elixir (W.F.S.)

℞
Spts Auranti — ℥ ii
" Cinnam — m
Alcohol — ℥ iv
Syr Simp
Aqua — aa — ℥ v

Simple Elixir. (Red) W.F.S.

℞
Simple Elix — ℥ XV.
Tr Cochineal Comp — ℥ ß
M

Elixir Calisaya (W.F.S.)

℞		
Tinct Cinchona	℥ iii	
Simp Elix		℥ xiii
M		

Syrup Ipecac (W.F.S.)

Fl Ext Ipecac	℥ viii	
Sp Vini Rect		℥ x
Aqua	O iii	℥ iv
Sacch Alb	lbs i	
M		

Andersons Scots Pills

℞		
Aloes	grs LX	
Sapo	grs X	
Colocynth		
Gamboge aa	grs iii	
Ol Anisi	gtts iii	
M ft Pil No XXIV		

Comp: Powder of Cochineal.
American Journal of Pharmacy 1874.

℞	
Cochineal	℥ ii
Alum	″
Potass Carb	″
″ Bi-tart	℥ iv
M	

Comp Tinct Cochineal

℞	
Comp Powder	℥ ij
Alco dil	℥ ij

Heat the dil alco slightly. add the powder and macerate 12 hours.

Carbolated Oil for Horses
(Dr Stocker)

℞	
Acid Carbolic	℥ ij
Glycerinae	℥ j
Tinct Aloes	℥ ij
40d Olive Oil	℥ iv

For Soda Water. to produce froth

Soap Bark	lbs. ij
Alcohol dilut	galls j

M. macerate 7 days

Mist Cretae. U.S.D. 1880

℞

Cretae Prep	℥ss Troy
Glycerine	f℥ss
Acacia Pulv	℈ grs 120
Aqua	
" Cinnamon aa	℥iv

M

Paregoric (Quick method)

℞

Tinct Opii	ʒiss
Glycerine	ʒij
Ol Anise	ʒi
Acid Benzoic	ʒi
Camphor	℈ii
Aqua	
Alcohol aa	Oi

Dissolve Ol Anise, Benz Acid & Camphor in the Alcohol
Mix the Tr Opii & Glycerine with the water then pour together and filter

℞
Pulv Cardamon
" Cochineal aa
" Cinnam
" Quassia aa
Glycerine
Alco dil Q.S.
Percolate 37½ pts and a

Tannate of Glycer

℞
Acid Tannic
Glycerine
Dissolve by means of water a

Oil Spike

℞
Petroleum
Oil Turbinth
" Amber
M

℞
Pulv Senna
" Liquorice aa
" Fennel Seed
" Sulphur aa
" Sugar
M

Cold Cream opt

℞
Cetaceum
Cera Alb
Oil Almonds dulc
Aqua Rosa
Sodae Boras
M

Glycerine Balm.

℞
Pulv Sod Bor
Glycerine
Aqua
M et perfume

℞
Bals Tolu ℥x
Finest Loaf Sugar Lbs 1¼
Aqua ℥x

Triturate the Bals Tolu with 8℥ Sugar then add the Aqua put in a bottle and macerate 48 hours with occasional agitation. then filter Crush. (not powder) the remainder of the sugar. place it in a percolator. and run the filtrate through.

Druggists Circular May 1887.

Hop Beer

℞
Hops 3/4 to 1 Lb
Malt Lbs 5.
Water 15 galls
Mollasses 1 gal
Sugar 2 cupfulls
Yeast 1 qt.
Yolks of 4 Eggs.

www.ingramcontent.com/pod-product-compliance
Lightning Source LLC
Chambersburg PA
CBHW032141080426
42733CB00008B/1164
* 9 7 8 3 7 4 2 8 2 3 2 6 7 *